NATIONAL GEOGRAPHIC

Ladders

AT THE MOVIES

GENRE **History Article**

Read to find out how movie-making has changed over time.

Fantasy Movies

by Jennifer Boudart

Movies transport us to magical worlds where animals talk, chocolate rivers flow, and dinosaurs rule.

1939 The Wizard of Oz

You know Dorothy and Toto are in Kansas because of the color on screen.

STORYLINE: Dorothy's dog Toto bites her mean neighbor. Fearing for Toto, Dorothy wants to run away. But a tornado hits Dorothy's house and knocks her out. Dorothy wakes up in the dazzling land of Oz. There she and Toto meet fantastic characters with familiar faces. Dorothy uses enchanted ruby slippers to get back home.

One look at the land of Oz told Dorothy she wasn't in Kansas anymore! Viewers knew, too, thanks to a visual clue—color! The Oz scenes were in full color, but the Kansas scenes were in shades of sepia brown.

To show Dorothy moving from Kansas to Oz, Dorothy's house was painted sepia. A stand-in actress wore a sepia dress, too. When the camera showed Oz, the "real" Dorothy was in full color. The contrast made Oz look fantastic.

1964
The Incredible Mr. Limpet

STORYLINE: Shy, awkward Henry Limpet learns he's not fit to join the Navy. His dreams are shattered. Henry wishes to become a fish. His wish comes true when he falls off a pier and becomes a fish! Henry likes his new life and even serves the Navy in his own special way.

The Incredible Mr. Limpet starred Don Knotts as Henry Limpet. The viewers saw Knotts only for the first 20 minutes. After Henry turned into a fish, Knotts was heard but not seen. Animators made Henry the fish look like Henry the human. His lips, eyes, glasses, and facial expressions were the same.

Artists animated the cartoon Henry and other undersea creatures. They painted frame-by-frame images on clear material called celluloid. They put each image on a

Here, Henry talks to Navy staff through a tool attached to the bottom of the ship. The tool is usually used to listen for submarines.

The animated Henry talks to his live friend George in this scene. Henry looks green when he's out of the water.

painted background. Then they photographed the series. When played back, the cartoons appeared to move. A movie, or motion picture, is a series of frame-by-frame images. The frames flash across the screen and our brains blend the images together. This creates an **optical illusion**, or something that looks different from what actually is. In movies, the optical illusion is nonstop motion.

The Incredible Mr. Limpet mixed live action with animation. When Henry surfaced to talk to his human friends, the movie featured both of them at the same time. The movie delivered humor, fantasy, romance, and suspense.

1971
Willy Wonka
& the Chocolate Factory

STORYLINE: A chocolate factory owner hides golden tickets in five chocolate bars. Those who buy the bars with the tickets can visit the factory. Charlie, who is very poor, finds a coin. He buys two candy bars and one of them has a golden ticket. He and his grandfather visit the factory. Their lives change forever.

"Inside this room, all of my dreams become realities. And some of my realities become dreams." Willy Wonka said this just before showing the Chocolate Room, the most magical part of his Chocolate Factory.

The Chocolate Room set for this movie was a sweet dream. Many props had edible materials! Chocolate ice cream mix was dumped into water to make a knee-deep chocolate river and waterfall. Giant mushrooms were filled with

In the movie, the actors were amazed when they entered the Chocolate Room. Their glee was real. It was the first time they'd actually seen it!

whipped cream. The giant lollipops were real, and Willy Wonka's teacup was made of spun sugar! Edible props created special challenges though. The chocolate river developed a sour stench. Special chemicals were needed to fix that. The waterfall foamed and turned the river white, so the crew added anti-bubble shampoo!

1982
E.T. the Extra-Terrestrial

^ Carlo Rambaldi spent about 5,000 hours creating the models for E.T.

STORYLINE: Elliot finds traces of an intruder in his shed. He uses a trail of candy to tempt the intruder to visit. The intruder is an alien whose spacecraft has left Earth. Elliot names the alien E.T., and they form a special bond. They work to get E.T. back home.

Steven Spielberg hired special-effects artist Carlo Rambaldi to design an alien for his movie.

Spielberg requested something "only a mother could love." Rambaldi created a stumpy creature with bulging eyes and gray wrinkled skin. Viewers fell in love with E.T.'s raspy voice, sweet facial expressions, and glowing fingertip.

Rambaldi built three E.T. models, with four interchangeable heads. One model was a suit worn by actors for full-body shots. The others were animatronics, or robotic puppets. Their controls guided E.T.'s 150 movements. E.T.'s motions ranged from raising a finger to wrinkling its nose and blinking its eyes. Off-camera puppeteers controlled these movements. A mime acted out scenes when the camera zoomed in on E.T.'s hands.

Elliot wore Halloween makeup and dressed up E.T. to help keep E.T. from being seen. Here, they watch for the spacecraft that's coming to get E.T.

1993

Jurassic Park

STORYLINE: **Theme park scientists have brought dinosaurs back to life. One worker steals their secret for growing dinosaurs. Then he turns off the electric fences that keep the dinosaurs under control. The *Tyrannosaurus rex* and *Velociraptors* start hunting each other—and the people.**

What sounds do dinosaurs make? Good question! Dinosaurs haven't been around for about 65 million years. So sound designers for *Jurassic Park* created dinosaur noises without knowing how dinosaurs sounded. They delivered a set of snorts, screeches, and roars.

The team blended walrus, dolphin, and seal sounds to create the *Velociraptors'* screams. For the roar of the *Tyrannosaurus rex*, they combined lion, tiger, alligator, and baby elephant sounds.

Jurassic Park won Academy Awards for Best Sound and Best Sound Effects.

Whale blowhole snorts and koala grunts created the *Tyrannosaurus rex's* heavy breathing. Mixed recordings of howler monkeys, rattlesnakes, hawks, and swans created the call of the *Dilophosaurus*.

Sound is a form of energy that travels in waves. *Jurassic Park* was the first movie to feature a surround-sound system called DTS Digital Sound™. Sound came through speakers around the theater. Special speakers **amplified** the energy of low sounds, such as dinosaur footsteps, to make them stronger. So moviegoers both heard and felt the energy of the dinosaur sounds!

2001–03
The Lord of the Rings

STORYLINE: A hobbit, who resembles a small man with large feet, finds a golden ring with special powers. The ring changes the hobbit into a strange creature known as Gollum that lives an unnaturally long life. Gollum loses the ring. Another hobbit finds the ring and learns of its incredible powers. He realizes the danger of keeping it, and gives it to others who set out to destroy it.

Huge battle scenes included very few live actors. Most soldiers were computer generated.

The Lord of the Rings movies were based on novels of the same title. They featured huge battle scenes with thousands of characters. Only a few were real! Most were computer-generated imagery (CGI) characters, or agents.

These agents could react without guidance during battles! They walked, ran, turned, and fought other agents. Using pre-programmed abilities, the agents were able to react to action, so they looked real.

The Lord of the Rings also featured a CGI creature named Gollum. Usually, actors pretend a CGI character is in a scene as they act. Computers add the character later. But the director hired Andy Serkis to perform Gollum's scenes so they'd be more believable. Serkis repeated each scene in a studio while cameras recorded his movements. A computer then built a CGI twin that copied Serkis' motions. Animators added details and laid the CGI Gollum over the image of Serkis in each scene.

The CGI Gollum sounds and acts a lot like Andy Serkis.

2011
Hugo

STORYLINE: After his father dies, Hugo hides in a train station. He sneaks out to steal meals and parts to rebuild a mechanical man his father wanted to fix. He makes friends with Isabelle, the goddaughter of a toyshop owner named Georges. The friends piece together secrets about the mechanical man and Georges' real identity.

Hugo featured 800-plus visual effects shots. Most used a "green screen" technique. Actors and objects were filmed against a solid green backdrop. Anything green on the film was later replaced with computer-generated images (CGI).

Old-fashioned movie tricks created some effects. Director Martin Scorsese wanted to honor pioneer moviemakers, including Georges Méliès, who was featured in the film. Scorsese used stop-action photography to animate a toy

The Paris cityscape behind Hugo is a CGI effect.

mouse. He shot hundreds of frames, adjusting the mouse's position a little each time. The mouse seemed to move when the frames played at normal speed.

Scorsese's mix of old and new paid off. *Hugo* won an Academy Award for Best Visual Effects.

Check In What are some movie-making techniques that changed over time? What are some that haven't changed?

GENRE Science Article

Read to find out how movies get their special sounds.

TRICKS for Sound

by Kathleen F. Lally

THE JOCKEY SNAPS THE REINS AND YELLS, "MOVE!" THE THUDDING OF THE HORSE'S HOOVES SPEEDS UP. ONLOOKERS CHEER!

Many sounds are used in a movie, but the only sound recorded during filming is dialogue. The rest are added after filming stops.

Sound is a form of energy that travels in waves. Engineers use **acoustics** to build movie sound studios. Acoustics involves how sound is made, how it travels, and how it is heard.

Artists often use a technique called "Foley" to create sounds. They work in rooms with props such as floors with different surfaces and pits with sand or gravel. Artists watch films and use objects or surfaces to make the sounds for each scene.

For the movie *Seabiscuit*, Foley artists might have created the thudding of hooves by pounding plungers stuffed with old rags on dirt piles. Snapping leather belts sound like reins snapping. A microphone near the Foley artists **amplifies** the sound and sends it to a recorder.

Foley artists walk, jump, move props, rub things, or break things to make sounds. They must exactly match the timing of their actions to those in the movie. Often, they use objects that are very different from the objects seeming to make the sounds in the movie. Check out these sounds and the Foley effects that could have made them.

Sound-makers are called Foley artists because of Jack Foley. This sound technician created sound effects for Universal Studios for more than 30 years. Adding sound effects in post-production was his idea. He mimicked the footsteps of actors. With a cane, he could step for two people at once! He reenacted the scenes so the sounds came at just the right moment. Although Jack Foley died in 1967, his artistry lives on.

For *The Water Horse*, Foley artists could have created the crackling sounds of a flaming fireplace...

...by crumpling cellophane candy wrappers.

For *Paulie*, Foley artists could have created the flapping sounds of bird wings…

…by slapping together a pair of leather gloves.

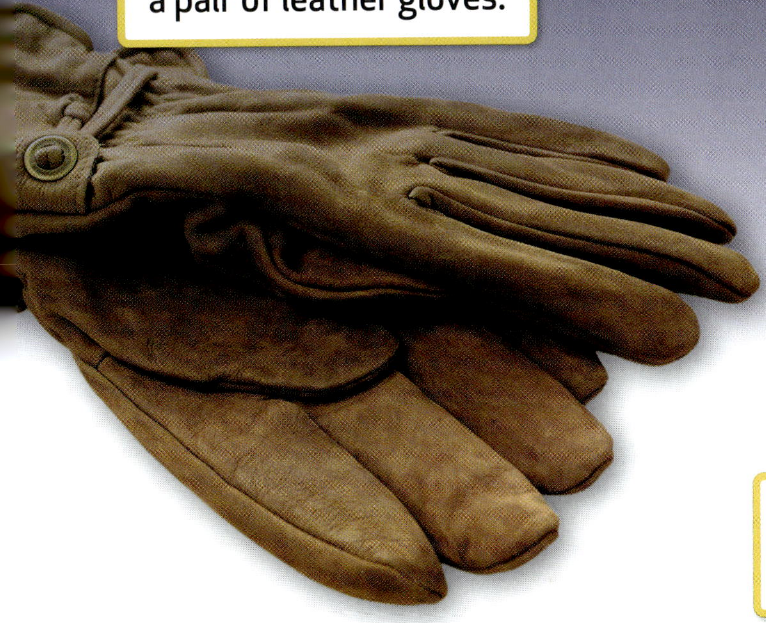

For *The Hobbit: An Unexpected Journey*, Foley artists could have created the sound of feet crunching dry grass and small twigs…

…by "walking" fingers across a bowl of uncooked rice.

Check In What are some ways Foley artists create sound effects?

GENRE Science Article

Read to find out how some kinds of special effects are created.

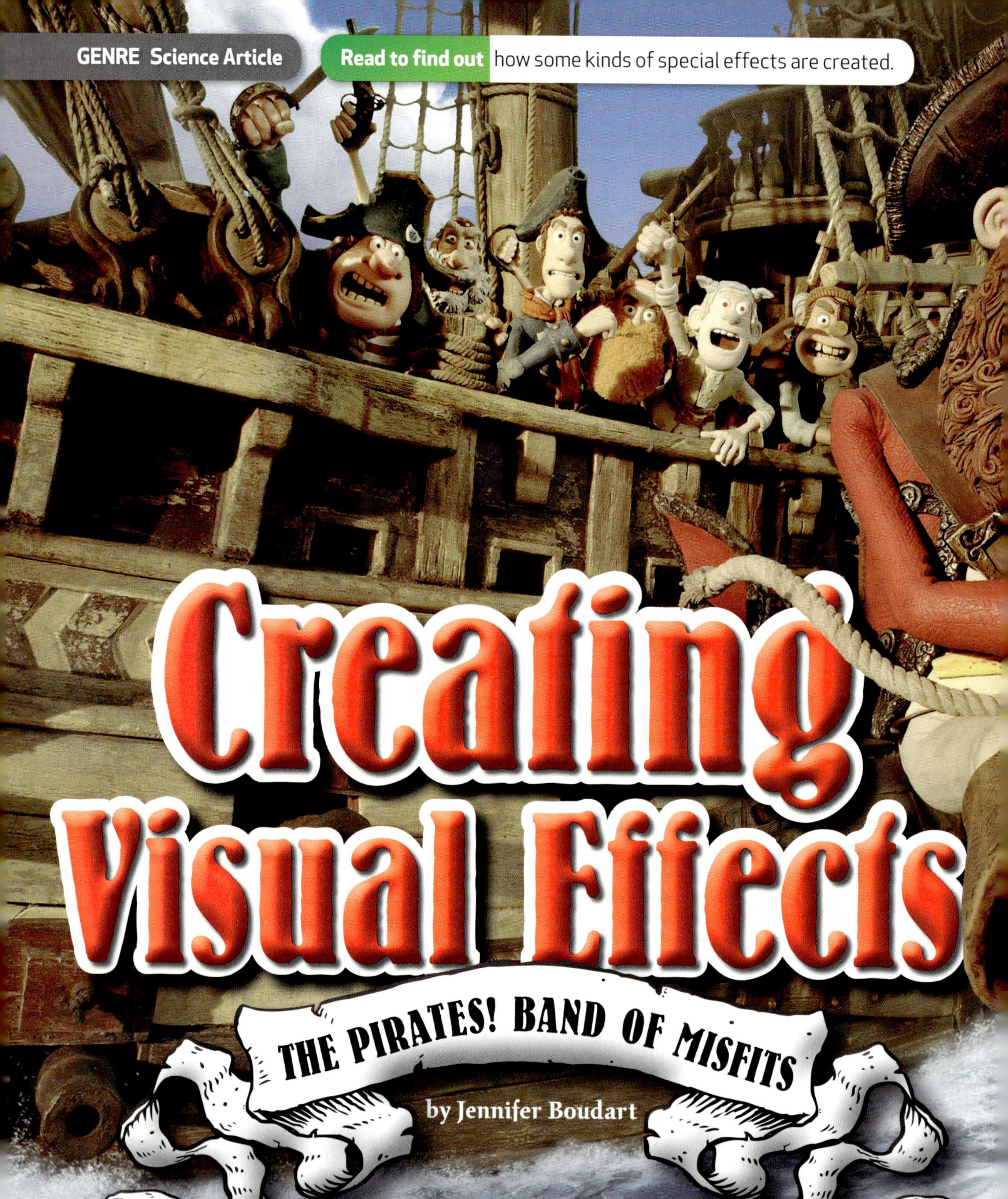

Creating Visual Effects

THE PIRATES! BAND OF MISFITS

by Jennifer Boudart

In the 2012 movie *The Pirates! Band of Misfits,* the pirate captain tries to become Pirate of the Year. It isn't easy. The captain and his goofy crew are more likely to find trouble than treasure!

The movie is animated, but its characters are actually three-dimensional puppets. An old-fashioned method called claymation brings them to life. This is a type of stop-motion animation. The puppets are made of clay. They are posed and photographed in a way that makes an **optical illusion,** or something that looks different from what actually exists. Here, the optical illusion is that of nonstop motion.

MAKING THE PUPPETS

The movie features 60-plus characters. Numerous moveable puppets were made for each character. They were produced in parts, such as clothing, torsos, heads, mouths, hands, hair, and eyebrows. Sculptors made certain parts from clay. Machines molded other parts from silicon, latex foam, or metal. Parts could be mixed and matched to create different poses or facial expressions. About 1,300 mouth shapes were made for the Captain alone! Why so many? Read on to find out.

MOVING THE PUPPETS

Stop-motion animators place a moveable model in a starting pose. They photograph it on a single frame of film. Then animators adjust the model's pose slightly. They may move a finger, curl a lip, or lift an eyebrow. Then they photograph the model in the new pose on the next frame. The animators continue adjusting and photographing the model frame-by-frame. When the film plays back at 24 frames per second, these images blend together in an optical illusion. The model appears to move, but the model is actually **static.** It lacks motion.

For *The Pirates! Band of Misfits*, animators saved time by switching mouths, eyebrows, and other parts rather than pinching and bending them between frames. Still, it was painstaking work, especially for scenes with groups of characters. One 90-second scene took three months to complete! Although the crew was able to work on up to 41 scenes at once, the 88-minute movie took 18 months to film.

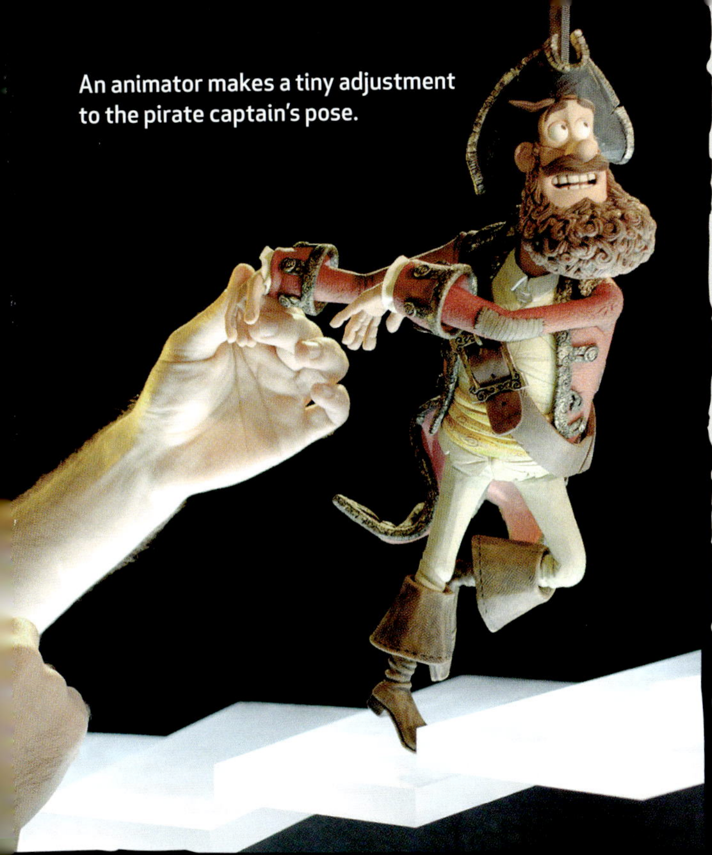

An animator makes a tiny adjustment to the pirate captain's pose.

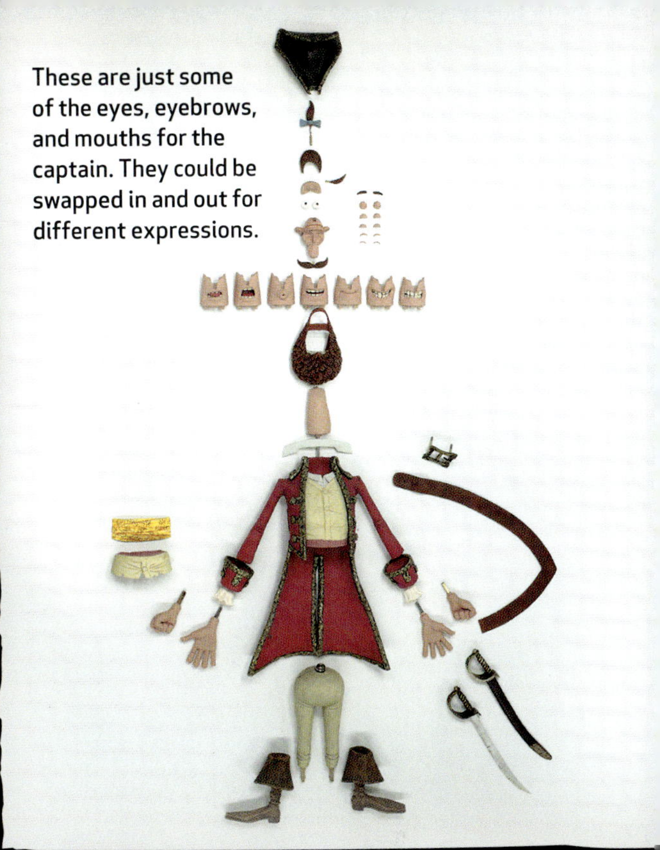

These are just some of the eyes, eyebrows, and mouths for the captain. They could be swapped in and out for different expressions.

A team of 33 animators worked on the movie.

SETTING THE SCENE

The characters also needed a world to live in. The story featured beaches, towns, theater stages, and the ship. Set designers built scenery and props with amazing attention to detail. The sets had to look good and also allow animators access to the puppets. Designers built a pirate ship that measured about 5 meters (15 feet) long and 6 meters (20 feet) high. Electric motors were placed under the ship and among its masts and sails. Their movements provided a sense of rocking waves and blowing winds.

Certain effects, such as splashing waves, were hard to create using stop-motion animation. So scenes were filmed in front of a green screen. The ocean, sky, and other backgrounds were added later as computer-generated images (CGI). But the movie's magic did not come from computers. It came from more than 300 people working together to make audiences fall in love with a cast partly made from clay.

The ship weighed over 350 kilograms (770 pounds)!

Director Peter Lord is known for his claymation movies.

Claymation brought the parrot to life, too.

Check In How does stop-motion animation work?

Read to find out how one movie made its way to giant IMAX screens.

IMAX® to the MAX

by Judy Elgin Jensen

Avatar is about an ex-soldier's fight to save the native people of the moon Pandora. People from Earth want to mine Pandora's resources, threatening its people. This 2009 movie generated a buzz. People thought its big budget and new computer-generated imagery (CGI) special effects would make it a blockbuster hit.

The movie's director hoped so. The film had taken over ten years to make and was said to have cost more than its $237,000,000 budget. It required totally new equipment and software to create the effects needed to bring the moon and its people to life. Over 1850 people worked on the visual effects alone!

In *Avatar,* the Na'vi people live on Pandora. They are tall with large eyes, pointed ears, and blue skin. A Na'vi language was created for the movie by a college professor.

Actor Sigourney Weaver played a scientist. Her character also had an avatar, right, that made her look like a Na'vi.

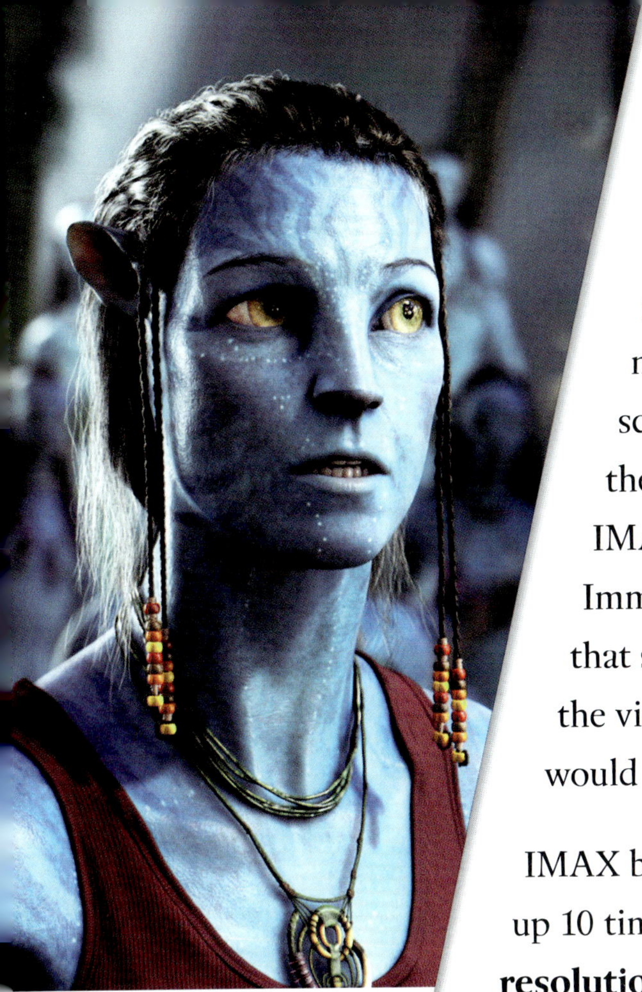

The director wanted *Avatar* to be a big hit on a big screen. That's why he got IMAX® involved. IMAX, or "image maximum," theaters had giant, curved screens and powerful sound. People felt they were in the middle of the action, which IMAX calls the "immersive" experience. Immerse can mean to "plunge into something that surrounds." The theaters would immerse the viewers in Pandora. This giant format would make the special effects pop.

IMAX blew *Avatar's* new special effects up 10 times in size. It gave the movie IMAX **resolution,** or high amount of image detail.

Avatar's action was 40 percent live and 60 percent CGI. Actors were filmed wearing motion capture suits with cameras mounted in front of their faces. This helped computers create exact CGI copies of the actors, so their expressions looked realistic. Added to the actors' CGI bodies were special Na'vi features, such as pointed ears, a tail, and blue skin.

Actors wearing special suits rode machines that moved while they were filmed. Their CGI characters used the same movements riding the flying CGI banshees.

The IMAX sound system floods the audience with sound from 44 speakers!

The camera captures two images of each shot, mimicking the left and right eye view. The two images are projected onto the screen. Viewers wear 3-D glasses that send the correct view to the correct eye, so objects seem to come off the screen.

IMAX screens are tall and wide. They curve beyond a viewer's vision, so the screen seems to have no end. A silver screen coating maximizes brightness and sharpness.

The IMAX® Effect

The three-dimensional, or 3-D, film *Avatar* impressed audiences. In 3-D films, flat screen images appear to have depth and "leap" off the screen. This method works because each eye sees a slightly different image. Combining the images gives the brain a sense of depth and distance. A 3-D movie tricks the eye into processing images this way.

Seats are at a steep angle, so all viewers are close and face the screen directly.

Check In What are some features of IMAX technology that make it a good format for the movie *Avatar*?

Discuss

1. How did the information in "Fantasy Movies" help you understand the other three pieces in the book?

2. What were some causes of the sound effects in "Tricks for Sound"? Make up two more sound effects yourself.

3. How were the optical illusions created in "Fantasy Movies" and "Creating Visual Effects" similar and how were they different?

4. Think about your favorite movie. What did you learn in this book that might help explain how your favorite movie was made?

5. What do you still wonder about how movies are filmed? What would be some good ways to find more information?